Finger Rhymes

Content-Connected Rhymes for Science, Math and Social Studies

Written by Lily Erlic

Illustrated by Veronica Terrill

Teaching & Learning Company

1204 Buchanan St., P.O. Box 10
Carthage, IL 62321-0010

This book belongs to

_____

Table of Contents

Dear Teacher or Parent,

Finger Rhymes is a resource guide for teachers and parents of children in grades preK-K. It is a book of poetry combined with fun movements. The adult should read the whole line, then read the action and present the action as well. The children should then mimic the action. This is a great way for children to move and explore science, math and social studies concepts at the same time.

The 10 themes included in the book reflect common early science, math and social studies. The themes are technology, outer space, colors, fruit, plant life cycle, animal life cycle, sharing, birthdays, other cultures and numbers. The "Technology" section reflects today's changing world. "Outer Space" gives children a feeling for the vastness of our world. "Colors" personifies colors in a comical sense. "Fruit" encourages good nutritional awareness in children. "Plant Life Cycle" gives children an appreciation for plant life. "Animal Life Cycle" encourages children to pretend to be animals growing. "Sharing" is one of my favorite sections because each rhyme is performed by a circle of children. "Birthdays" is all about celebrating each individual child. "Other Cultures" shows a cultural and social awareness and helps children learn about differences. "Numbers" incorporates early math and rhyming to make counting fun.

These themes can provide enrichment during gym, science, math or social studies lessons. This resource guide gives you the opportunity to transform classroom lessons into live action!

Sincerely,

Lily Erlic

Computer World

What if the computer was a dream?
(Place hands under head like you are sleeping)

What would we do? How would it seem?
(Shrug shoulders)

Put your head down and close your eyes,
(Place head down and close eyes)

Let's dream of a computer surprise.
(Put hands up in surprise)

Let's dream about the keyboard and type away,
(Pretend to type)

Let's dream about all the games to play.
(Place hands under head)

Then think of family things to do,
(Point to head)

With Mom, Dad, Sister and Brother too.
(Point to everyone)

Your family can play a fun computer game,
(Pretend to type on a keyboard)

*Are there any you can name?
(Let children think of games. You can suggest math, spelling or story games.)

*The asterisk indicates "discussion time" between adults and children.

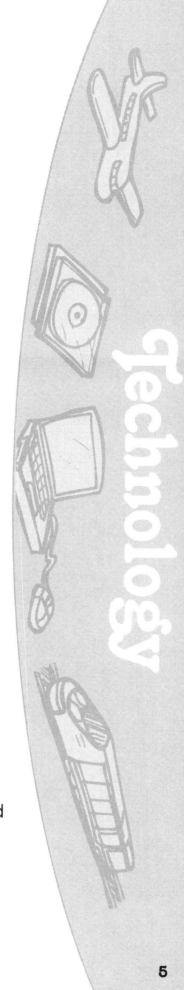

Chunnel

Discuss what the "Chunnel" is with children. The Chunnel is a tunnel that goes under the ocean and connects England and France.

Have you ever been in a tunnel that is under the ocean,
(Make tunnel shape with hands)

Where there are cars and trains and lots of commotion?
(Look through your hand tunnel)

It's under the channel between England and France.
(Show children on a map or point with fingers in the air)

Have you ever been there? Have you had the chance?
(Lift shoulders)

Let's go there, just you and me.
(Point to children then yourself)

Let's go there. What will we see?
(Place hands above eyes)

Let's hop into our car and drive in through;
(Hop)

Buckle the seat belts and turn on the lights too.
(Pretend to buckle seat belts)

Hold on to the wheel and be sure to drive straight;
("Drive" across room)

Keep the wheel steady and concentrate.
(Hold onto a "wheel")

There are bright lights all around
(Stretch arms up)

To guide us through underground.
(Make tunnel shape with hands)

Can you hear water dripping like rain?
(Place hands over ears and wiggle fingers)

I think the tunnel is leaking again!
(Wiggle fingers in front like water droplets)

The engineers will fix the crack
(Pound fists)

While we eat our special snack.
(Pretend to eat with hands)

Let's leave the tunnel and park our car,
(Pretend to park car)

Unbuckle our seat belts and say "that was far!"
(Pretend to unbuckle belts and wipe forehead)

Technology

The Spinning CD

The spinning CD moves around and around.
(Spin body around)

It spins slowly, then quickly without a sound.
(Spin slowly, then quickly)

Pretend you're a CD flying through space.
(Extend arms)

Travel quickly to another time and place.
(Run quickly to a new place in the room)

We pass stars and comets and the sun.
(Point)

We are having so much fun.
(Make laughing sounds)

We land on a planet far away
(Stop)

In a puddle of gooey clay.
(Pretend to step out of a puddle of clay)

Let's build a tower oh so high
(Extend arm up)

That it nearly touches the sky!
(Reach as high as possible)

Let's spin back through space
(Spin around)

To return to our place!
(Stop)

We're the spinning CD that moves around and around,
(Spin around)

We spin slowly, then quickly, without a sound!
(Spin slowly, then quickly and stop)

Sky Train

All aboard! Let's board the train, you and I;
(Jump)

Let's board the train that's near the sky.
(Point up)

Let's sit in our seats and hang on tight,
(Make fists on side of body)

For this is like an airplane flight.
(Spread arms out)

Look through the window and all around;
(Place hands above eyebrows)

We're on the train and city bound.
(Extend arm in front of body)

The journey is smooth, like going down a slide.
(Pretend to slide)

It is a short, but glorious ride.
(Place hands in air)

Our ride curves, but mostly goes straight.
(Run around room in different directions)

Now we have arrived at our gate.
(Wipe forehead)

Let's step out before they close the door.
(Step and jump)

Someday we'll come back for more!
(Put hands up to look for the next train)

Technology

Airplane Ride

Ask children if they have ever flown on an airplane. Describe an airplane ride so children who have not been on one can understand the poem.

Flying over the ocean, flying over the sea,
(Extend arms out and move around room)

Flying on an airplane, just you and me.
(Point to children and yourself)

Bouncing on the airplane, bouncing in my seat,
(Jump)

Asking for a treat that's sweet.
(Make chewing motions)

Looking out the window at the city below,
(Shade eyes with hands)

Watching the scenery, what a show!
(Clap)

The cars look like tiny ants;
(Crouch down)

The houses look smaller than cats.
(Stretch like a cat)

The clouds look like marshmallow pies,
(Rub tummy)

And the sun is shining in my eyes.
(Close eyes)

On the airplane, we're flying high,
(Spread arms)

Flying an airplane to kiss the sky!
(Repeat twice, blow kisses)

Technology

Mars

I'm the planet called Mars.
(Point to yourself)

I'm the brightest among the stars.
(Point to the ceiling)

Let's pretend I'm a planet ball.
(Make a round circle with fingers)

Throw me around; don't let me fall!
(Throw pretend ball around)

I'm very red and very hot,
(Make sizzling noises)

And if you drop me, you'll have to trot.
(Pretend to drop the ball)

Trot like a horse around the room,
(Move around room in a trotting motion)

Until I say the magic word: *BOOM!*
*(Say "boom" for the children to stop. Say "trot"
for them to move. Repeat several times).*

Outer Space

Pass the Pluto!

Show the class where Pluto is in the solar system. Each child needs a small ball. Use a small gray ball to represent Pluto.

I am Pluto. I am very small.
(Point to yourself, crouch down)

I'm little—like a teeny, tiny ball.
(Make a fist or lift ball up and stretch arm)

I'm very far away from the heat of the sun,
(Keep stretching)

But even though I'm chilly, I can still be fun!
(Dance with the ball)

Bounce me low, bounce me high,
(Make bounce actions with ball)

Bounce me right up to the sky!
(Bounce ball once toward ceiling)

Bounce me to a friend or toss me up,
(Children may choose what to do)

Throw me around or drop me in a cup.
(Have buckets handy to use as cups)

Roll me around in a circle on the floor,
(Trace an imaginary circle with ball)

Hold me in your hand and soar, soar, soar
(Move around room)

Just like a rocket that is shooting through the air,
(Keep moving with the ball in hand)

Or a space shuttle ride at the county fair!
(Pretend to ride in a space shuttle)

I'm sorry to say it's time for me to say good-bye
(Sit down on floor with ball)

And go back to the solar system with all my friends in the sky!
(Place balls back in storage area)

Moonrise

Children can use helium balloons for this poem or the teacher can use one to demonstrate. If the children are using real balloons, be sure the balloon string is attached to each child's wrist. Or the whole class, including the teacher, can have pretend balloons.

Let's fly up to the moon
(Spread and flap arms)

By holding the string of a balloon.
(Hold balloon)

The balloon will let us float up high,
(Stretch body towards ceiling)

Beyond the clouds and through the sky.
(Wave balloon back and forth)

We'll land on the moon that looks like cheese,
(Jump)

Keep holding the balloon and sit on your knees.
(Sit on knees)

Smell the ground; try not to sneeze,
(Bend down to floor and sniff)

Then take a bite to see if it's cheese.
(Pretend to take a bite from floor)

Hold on to the balloon with all your might;
(Hold string with both hands)

We have to pass by stars and rockets tonight.
(Run around room with balloon)

The moon is gone because now it's day;
(Pretend to search for the moon)

Let go of your balloon, and watch it fly away.
(Let go of balloon or pretend balloon)

Outer Space

Ring Around Saturn

Children need a Hula-Hoop™ for this action rhyme. If none are available, create a large cardboard Hula-Hoop™ for each child.

I'm the planet Saturn with a ring around my middle.
(Look down at Hula-Hoop™ and move it from side to side)

When I spin around, it sounds like music from a fiddle.
(Try twirling the Hula-Hoop™ around yourself)

Place the ring above your head,
(Stretch arms up holding hoop)

Set it down for a bed.
(Place it on floor and pretend to nap)

Twirl it on the floor like a top;
(Twirl like a top: hold it upright and spin)

Watch it turn, then let it stop.
(Stop the hoop)

Place it around your middle and run, run and run!
(Run to a new spot in the room)

Now pretend you're spinning around the sun!
(Have children walk in a circle around the room)

Sunshine Music

I'm the sun way up in the sky.
(Point to the ceiling)

You can't reach me, even if you fly.
(Flap arms up and down)

As time passes, I move across the land,
(Move across the room)

And play music like a marching band.
(Pretend to play musical instruments)

My music plays when I shine on the trees,
(Stand tall like a tree)

In the fall when I dry out the leaves,
(Pick up pretend leaves and throw)

In the spring when I help flowers grow,
(Pretend to smell flowers)

In the winter when I melt the snow,
(Move fingers back and forth like falling snow)

And in the summer when I warm up the night,
(Spread arms widely)

Even though it's dark and I'm out of sight!
(Let the children hide or tuck their heads)

Outer Space

Playful Blue

Show children the color blue, such as a blue piece of paper or a blue object. The teacher could also wear blue for the lesson.

I'm the color of the sky;
(Point up)

I'm also the color of some people's eyes.
(Point to eyes)

Do you know who I am from the clues?
(Point to head)

That's right! I'm the color blue!
(Show something blue to the class)

You can see me in a swimming pool;
(Move arms in a swimming motion)

You can see me in an icicle, so cool.
(Pretend to hold icicle in hand)

You can see me in a blue jay flying high;
(Fly like a bird around the room)

You can see me covering the sky.
(Point to the ceiling or sky)

I'm a ribbon for best-in-show,
(Raise heads in air like you won something)

And a part of the rainbow.
(Arch your whole body and touch hands to floor)

I'm the color blue,
(Show blue object again)

And I liked playing with you!
(Cheer and clap)

Green Scene

Show the class the color green, such as a green piece of paper or a green object.

Suggested Activity: Take children outside or look through a window to name things that are green.

I'm the color green.
(Point to self)

Where can I be seen?
(Point around room)

You can see me in the trees,
(Stand tall like a tree)

Or in the grass that grows so free.
(Feel or pretend to feel grass)

You can see me in the leaves that fall,
(Pretend to jump in leaves)

Or the flowers that grow so tall.
(Point up)

You can see me when you're stirring pea soup,
(Pretend to stir)

Or when you're playing with your green Hula-Hoop™.
(Sway hips around)

I'm not a color that likes to hide;
(Hide eyes behind hands)

I'm all around when you look outside!
(Spread arms)

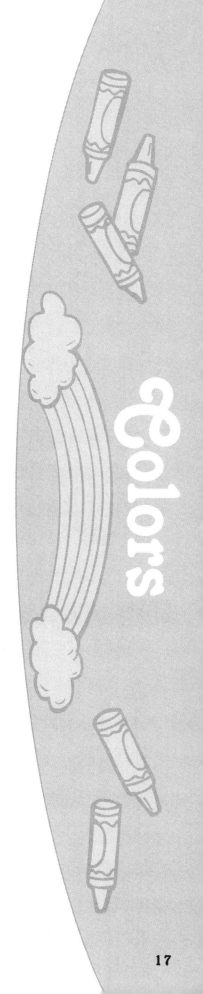

Yellow Days

I'm the yellow sun high in the sky;
(Stretch arms up)

I shine all day and make things dry.
(Wave arms back and forth)

I shrivel grapes and tomatoes too,
(Roll body up like a ball)

And make sparkles in the water so blue.
(Open and close hands)

I make flowers grow tall and strong,
(Stretch arms up)

And listen to the crickets sing their song.
(Place hand to ear and pretend to listen)

I see people tanning on the beach;
(Lie down on a mat)

They yawn and stretch and try to reach
(Yawn)

My warm, yellow rays,
(Stretch arms out)

And hope that I will stay all day.
(Pretend to hug the sun)

And when it's time for me to say good night,
(Place head on hands)

I sink below the horizon and out of sight!
(Crouch down, tuck head under arms)

Colors

Brown Around Town

Place a brown piece of paper on the wall or bring a brown object to show.

I'm the color of tree bark.
(Point to yourself)

I'm also the color of chocolate that's dark.
(Ask the children to guess)

That's right! I'm the color brown;
(Point to yourself)

You've probably seen me around the town.
(Point around the room)

I'm the color of dry leaves in the fall,
(Pretend to jump in leaves)

And you can see me at the mall.
(Hands to eyes as if searching)

I'm in the house that's built for two.
(Outline house with hands around body)

I'm in the boat with a crew.
(Pretend to row a boat)

I'm the color of the doghouse that's built outside;

I'm the color of the dog who wants to hide,
(Hide behind your hand)

Yes, I'm the color brown;
(Point to yourself)

You can see me all around town!
(Point around room)

Colors

Pink, I Think!

I'm the color of a rose,
(Pretend to smell a rose)

What color am I do you suppose?
(Have children guess the color)

What do you think?
(Keep guessing)

That's right! I'm the color pink!
(Show a pink object)

Let's move around like a pink flamingo,
(Lift knees up high and walk)

And make footprints all in a row.
(Walk in a line across room)

Lick your fingers after you eat shrimp,
(Lick fingers)

Grab the pink lemonade and take a sip.
(Pretend to drink)

What else is pink?
(Shrug shoulders)

What do you think?
(Ask children for suggestions)

Let's pretend we're a pink car.
(Pretend to step into vehicle)

We'll drive away, but not too far.
(Move around room making car sounds)

Let's get pink cotton candy at the fair,
(Pretend to eat the cotton candy)

And look at the pigs, but be sure not to stare!
(Shake your finger)

Let's fish for pink salmon in the light of day,
(Stretch arms back and then forward like a fishing rod)

Then eat strawberry ice cream as we go on our way,
(Pretend to lick ice-cream cone)

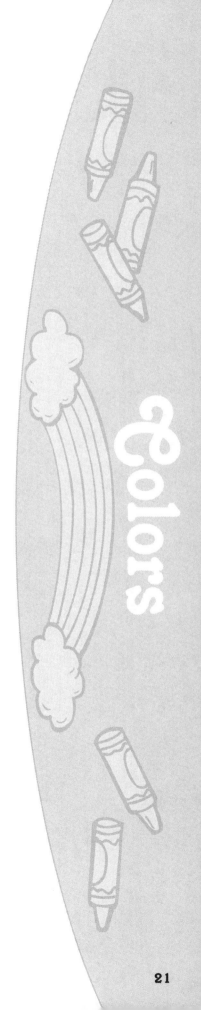

Orange Spice

I'm a little orange rolling around;
(Make a fist, roll fist around in the air)

I can bounce on my branch without a sound.
(Move fist up and down)

Plop! In the basket I go,
(Make a basket with left hand, place fist in basket)

Off to market with Farmer Joe.
(Make walking motion with fingers)

Someone buys me and puts me in a sack.
(Continue walking with fingers)

She peels me and eats me for a healthy snack.
(Pretend to peel an orange)

A sprinkle of cinnamon, cloves and nutmeg makes Orange
 Spice,
(Shake fist three times in the air)

And now I taste twice as nice!
(Smack or lick lips)

I'm a little orange spice jumping around,
(Make a fist, move fist up and down)

I can bounce down your tummy without a sound!
(Move fist up and down)

Apple Sack

Let's pick an apple from the apple tree;
(Pretend to pick an apple)

Bite into it: one, two, three.
(Pretend to bite into an apple three times)

Now be an apple rolling down a hill,
(Roll on mats)

Slow, slower, fast and faster until
(Move slow and fast)

We hit a rock and bounce up high
(Jump)

Like a bird that wants to fly.
(Flap arms)

We'll fall into the stream and float,
(Crouch down)

Like a wobbly old boat,
(Wobble back and forth on your feet)

Until a fisherman reels us in.
(Pretend to reel in a fish)

Then through the air we'll spin
(Twirl)

As the fisherman throws us back
(Run backwards)

Into a big brown apple sack.
(Jump and crouch)

Fruit

Banana Slide

I'm a banana sliding down the street,
(Pretend to slide on floor)

Smiling and waving at the people I meet.
(Wave)

I'm jumping and hopping along
(Jump and hop)

While dancing and singing my song:
(Dance)

"I'm a banana: one, two, three;
(Show three fingers)

I like to skip and hop you see.
(Skip and hop)

I like to jump and I like to dance,
(Jump and dance)

I like to stretch and I like to prance.
(Stretch and prance)

I'm very tall, but not very wide;
(Stretch arms up and to the sides)

I like to swing and I like to slide.
(Move body back and forth, pretend to slide)

I'm a banana: one, two, three;
(Show three fingers)

Come skip and hop with me!"
(Skip and hop)

Fruit

Lemon Time

I'm a lemon; I grow on a tree.
(Make a tree shape with hands)

Yellow like the sun is the color of me.
(Make a circle with hands)

If you open me up, you'll see
(Place hands together, then open)

Juice and seeds inside of me.
(Point to self)

Mix my juice with water and honey too,
(Pretend to stir)

Then pour a drink of lemonade for you!
(Pretend to share and drink)

Fruit

Grape Jelly in My Belly

I like to pick grapes, bunch after bunch;
(Reach up, pretend to pick grapes)

I'll eat some for breakfast, dinner and lunch.
(Rub tummy)

I put them in my basket and carry them around,
(Place grapes in basket)

Then take some to the market to sell them in town.
(Run across room)

I'll earn lots of money and put it away,
(Pretend to place money in pocket)

For jars and sugar to make grape jelly today.
(Rub tummy)

We mix it all together in a great big pot.
(Stir)

I can't taste it now because it's very hot.
(Shake finger)

When it's ready, I'll taste it with a spoon,
(Pretend to taste jelly)

And eat it with toast on a sunny afternoon.
(Spread pretend jelly)

Fruit

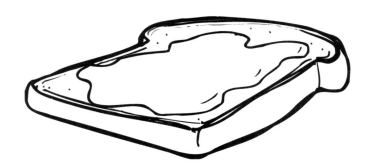

The Lettuce Leaves

I planted a seed to grow into a plant;
(Place thumb and forefinger together, then touch floor)

The seed was no bigger than a tiny ant.
(Place thumb and forefinger together)

I watered my plant and gave it some food,
(Pretend to pour water)

And patted the leaves in a happy mood.
(Pat the air)

The leaves shook and began to wave;
(Shake body and wave arms)

They said, "It's dark in here, like a cave!"
(Put hands in front of eyes)

The sun was shining with all its might,
(Put arm in circle above head)

So I put them in the sun and they enjoyed the light.
(Look happy)

My plant was happy as I pulled off some leaves;
(Pretend to pull leaves)

They said, "Where are you taking us, please?"
(Extend arms)

I'm making a salad with tomatoes too,
(Pretend to toss salad)

That I want to share with you!
(Point to children)

Plant Life Cycle

The Onion Underground

I planted some onion bulbs in the fall;
(Pretend to plant bulbs)

I counted five onion bulbs in all.
(Count 1-5 with fingers)

I put them in and covered them up,
(Pretend to push and cover with soil)

Patted the soil and watered them from a cup.
(Pat floor and pretend to water)

The days passed and the green onions grew tall.
(Stand tall and stretch)

When they were ready, I picked them all.
(Count 1-5 with fingers)

I washed the onions with a hose,
(Pretend to wash with hose)

Then I smelled them with my nose.
(Smell)

They smelled so good, I took a big bite.
(Pretend to bite)

I had bad breath that night.
(Cover mouth)

My friends ate some onions too;
(Pretend to chew)

We put them in our homemade stew!
(Rub tummy)

Carrot Crop

When I was a farmer not long ago,
(Pretend to garden)

I planted carrots all in a row.
(Pretend to plant seeds in a row)

My friends and I pulled them out one by one.
(Pretend to pull the carrots)

They were so big and seemed to weigh a ton.
(Pretend to carry something heavy)

When we pulled them from the ground,
(Pull)

We cut carrot slices that were round.
(Pretend to slice)

One carrot slice became a steering wheel,
(Hold pretend carrot slice in front of you)

And we drove around the carrot field.
(Drive around room)

We went between all the rows,
(Drive up and down the room)

Over carrot tops and around the hoes.
(Jump)

We made another carrot slice into a hat,
(Place on head)

And we danced around and scared the cat.
(Dance, wiggle and giggle)

When the sun went down, we took the carrots from our heads,
(Pretend to take carrot off head)

And made them into pillows for our cozy little beds.
(Place head on hands)

Plant Life Cycle

The Bean Team

Once there were five old beans,
(Hold up five fingers)

They were wrinkled, nasty and mean.
(Make a mean face)

The first one said, "Let's go this way.
(Move around room)

We need to get planted today!"
(Crouch down)

The second one said, "Who will plant us in the ground?"
(Shrug shoulders)

The third one said, "There is no one around!"
(Use hand to look for someone)

The fourth one said, "Look over there!"
(Point)

There was a farmer with braids in her hair.
(Pretend to braid hair)

The fifth one said, "I need the earth to be my bed;
(Lie down)

It's this cold I really dread."
(Hug self)

The farmer picked up all five beans,
(Show five fingers)

And placed them in a pocket of her jeans.
(Pretend to put beans in pocket)

She planted the beans in the sun,
(Pretend to plant)

And they began to have some fun.
(Pretend to be happy)

By the window, the beans grew tall,
(Stretch body)

They weren't mean any more at all.
(Big smile)

Tomato Vines

Tomatoes grow on a long vine,
(Stretch body)

They are twisted and intertwined.
(Twist body)

At first, they are small and green,
(Crouch)

But then they grow tall and lean.
(Stretch body)

We'll tie them against a pole
(Pretend to tie)

So they don't fall down too low.
(Fall to floor)

When they're ripe and ready,
(Jump)

Hold the branch steady.
(Stretch arms in front of body)

Take the fruit in your hand,
(Open hand)

Pull it gently, slowly and
(Pull)

Bite it so the juice drips down
(Pretend to bite)

On your fingers and all around!
(Spread fingers)

Plant Life Cycle

Wobbly Colt

When I was a colt, my legs would wobble and wiggle;
(Wobble legs back and forth)

Like gelatin in a bowl, my legs would jiggle.
(Jiggle legs)

Each day, I tried to walk straight and steady,
(Walk in a line unsteadily)

But I kept falling. I just wasn't ready!
(Fall to floor)

My mother kept saying, "Try again!"
(Rise and fall)

I didn't think I could do it, but then,
(Look sad)

I stood straight and strong like a tree.
(Stand tall)

I walked straight and I felt free,
(Walk straight)

Free like a bird that learns to fly,
(Spread arms pretend to fly)

Free like a cat that likes to spy.
(Place hands on face and peak through fingers)

When I was a colt, my legs would wobble and wiggle,
(Wobble legs back and forth)

Like gelatin in a bowl, my legs would jiggle.
(Jiggle legs)

Animal Life Cycle

Mouse in the House

There once was a tiny mouse
(Use thumb and forefinger to show tiny)

Who lived in a tiny house.
(Make house outline with body)

His tiny house was behind a wall,
(Put arms together to make a wall)

And was smaller than a ball.
(Use arms to make a circle)

The tiny mouse
(Use fingers to show tiny)

Liked to run around the house.
(Jog around room)

He would hide under the bed,
(Crawl)

And shake his tail and his head.
(Shake body)

In the kitchen, he would eat the cheese,
(Pretend to eat)

But first, he would always say "Please."
(Yell "please" as a group)

He would run behind the broom,
(Race around room)

And get stuck and yell to the room.
(Shake)

Animal Life Cycle

"Help, help!" he would say
(Yell "help" as a group)

As he twisted and wiggled all day.
(Wiggle body)

When he managed to get free,
(Jump for joy)

He would climb the fridge like a tree.
(Pretend to climb)

Then he would eat some cheese,
(Pretend to eat)

But first, he would always say "Please."
(Yell "please" as a group)

He'd eat cheddar, mozzarella and brie,
(Rub tummy)

And would share some with you and me!
(Point to children, then self)

As he ate the cheese, he'd say,
(Move mouth)

"Cheese will help us grow big one day!"
(Stand tall)

Animal Life Cycle

A Cow's Life

There once was a cow named Jo

Who liked to count flowers and toes.
(Count)

When she walked through the field of green,
(Walk across room)

The other cows would laugh and be mean.
(Make mean face)

Jo continued to count all day,
(Count)

Until a large bull got in her way.
(Jump)

The bull chased her around the green field,
(Run around room)

Until Jo found a fence for a shield.
(Hide behind pretend fence)

"Why are you chasing me?" asked poor Jo,
(Shrug shoulders)

The bull replied, "We're tired of your counting, you know!"

Then the bull jumped over the fence,
(Jump)

And said, "This is all nonsense!"
(Shake finger)

"Let's make a deal;

You'll only count after meals."
(Pretend to shake hands)

Then Jo said, "That will be fine,

Although I like to count all the time!"
(Look sad)

Then Jo wrote a counting book
(Pretend to read)

That made the cows take another look.
(Look around)

They smiled and were happy to see,
(Smile)

That Jo counted them as well as you and me!
(Count all the children)

The Chick's Eggshell

In an eggshell is where I live,
(Lie on floor in a ball)

I'm trying to break free so a push I give.
(Push arms up)

"Help me! Help me! I feel like a clam,
(Move arms around)

But I'm not. Can you guess what I am?"
(Have children guess who is in the eggshell)

Yes, you're right! I'm a baby chick.

I cracked my shell; it was quite a trick.
(Jump and drop to floor)

Now I'm free; I can run around.
(Run)

I can even touch the ground.
(Touch floor)

The other chicks are following me;
(Let children form a line and walk around room)

We hop over the tiny stones we see.
(Hop)

What else should we do?

Sure, we'll eat our feed too.
(Pretend to eat off the floor)

We jump and hop in the hay,
(Jump and hop)

And roll in the mud and stomp in the clay.
(Stomp)

We run in circles around the barn,
(Run in circles)

And play and get tangled in yarn.
(Move arms up and down as if tangled)

We flap our wings like a butterfly,
(Flap arms)

And sneak a bite of apple pie.
(Pretend to peck)

The farmer's wife shoos us away,
(Wave hands)

But she knows we'll be back another day!
(Walk sneakily)

Kitten Purrs

I'm a tiny kitten licking some cream;
(Pretend to lick)

I'm part of a kitten licking team.
(Lick)

We licked to the left and then to the right;
(Turn left then right and lick)

We licked all day and all of the night.
(Stand tall, then place head down while licking)

But we got tired and we had to quit,
(Sit)

So we read a book and had to sit.
(Pretend to read)

Kittens purring filled the room
(Make purr sounds)

Like a flower opening to bloom.
(Spread arms)

We purred to the left and then to the right;
(Turn left, then right and purr)

We purred all day and all of the night.
(Stand tall, then place head down while purring)

We decided to create a purring team;
(Join hands)

We purred in the sun and to a moonbeam.
(Make purring sounds)

We became cats as big as a pillow.
(Grow by slowly standing up)

Our home was underneath a willow.
(Dangle arms)

We dangled and purred from every branch;
(Pretend to climb tree, then purr)

To hear our song was quite a catch.
(Pretend to listen)

We purred to the left and then to the right,
(Turn left, then right and purr)

We purred all day and all of the night!
(Stand tall, then place head down while purring)

Sharing Sun

Teach sharing with these circle time rhymes. Have children hold hands to form a circle for each rhyme. Children pretend to feel and share the warmth of the sun in this first rhyme. What does the sun share with us?

Let's make a circle like the sun
(Hold hands and form a circle)

That shares its light 'til the day is done.
(Raise hands)

Its rays shine up and down,
(Raise hands up, then down)

And all over the streets of the town.
(Point around room)

The rays shine through the sky,
(Stretch arms up)

And on the birds that love to fly.
(Move around room like a bird)

It shines on the houses and the trees,
(Make arms look like tree branches)

It shines on the lake and the leaves.
(Shake arms and pretend to drop leaves)

Its rays shine up and down,
(Raise hands up, then down)

Golden like a king or queen's crown.
(Point to head)

Then the sun will go to sleep,
(Place hands beside face and bend head)

Below the horizon, slowly without a peep!
(Bend knees, then lie down in the circle)

Christmas Tree Circle

The teacher may provide a real Christmas tree to place in the center of the circle, or suggest an imaginary tree to children.

Let's make a circle around the Christmas tree,
(Hold hands and form a circle)

And walk around it on our knees.
(Walk on knees around tree)

It looks so tall; it looks so grand;
(Stand up tall like the Christmas tree)

Let's walk around it with our hands.
(Bend over, try to walk with hands)

And when we turn the lights off and on,
(Make hands open and close)

We can listen to a Christmas song.
(Play or sing a Christmas song)

When we hear those songs play,
(Pretend to play piano with fingers)

We'll pretend to be carolers on our way,
(Open mouth as if singing)

Singing Christmas songs around the tree,
(Hold hands around the tree)

So all can hear us singing happily!
(Sing Christmas songs with the children)

Sharing

Marshmallow Roast

Suggestion: Play a campfire song in the background.

Let's sit around the campfire with our sticks,
(Pretend to hold campfire sticks)

Roasting our marshmallows until they're thick.
(Place arms in front of your body to form a circle)

They are gooey, golden and sweet,
(Move fingers back and forth)

And they are good enough to eat!
(Place hands to mouth)

Let's clap and move our feet,
(Clap and move feet)

To the rhythm and the beat.
(Listen to the music)

We'll sing a happy campfire song,
(Listen, put hands behind ears)

And move our bodies right along.
(Dance)

Wait! I hear an animal moving around.
(Make animal sounds with children)

Can you tell me about the sound?
(Ask children what kind of sound they hear)

Is it a bear, a squirrel or a deer?
(Make these animal sounds)

What kind of sounds do you hear?
(Listen)

Sharing

TLC10546 Copyright © Teaching & Learning Company, Carthage, IL 62321-0010

Is it a bear moving like this?
(Curve arms and move like a bear)

Or a bird looking for a kiss?
(Flap arms and blow a kiss)

Is it a rabbit hopping around?
(Hop)

Or a squirrel jumping up and down?
(Jump)

But now we'll move our feet
(Shuffle feet)

To the rhythm and the beat!
(Listen to music)

Sharing a Pear!

Once I had an apple and a pear,
(Pretend to hold fruit)

That I wanted to share.
(Extend arms)

I cut the fruit in two—
(Place two fingers up)

Some for me and some for you!
(Point to self and to a friend)

The Fish in the Middle

Let's make an ocean with our hands,
(Make a circle with children)

And keep the water in as best we can.
(Tighten the circle together)

Watch the fish swimming around,
(Ask a few children to be fish swimming in the circle)

Wiggling their tails without a sound.
(Move bodies)

They swim and shake and try to get out,
(Shake and try to swim through the circle)

Because there is a shark after them! They shout,
"Help! Get us out of here!"

(Fish go back to the circle, and other children become fish. Then repeat lines above making sure all the children have had a turn being a fish.)

Birthdays Are Special Days!

A birthday is a special day;
(Wave hands in excitement)

Birthdays are a time to play—
(Point to imaginary watch on wrist)

Throwing balloons up in the air,
(Pretend to throw balloons)

Putting ribbons in your hair,
(Rub hands through hair)

Jumping over party hats,
(Jump)

Swinging upside down like bats,
(Bend body over, then swing arms)

Waving streamers all around,
(Wiggle arms)

Like squirming snakes on the ground.
(Wiggle bodies on the floor)

Birthdays are a time to bake,
(Pretend to place cake in oven)

And blow out candles on the cake.
(Blow out pretend candles)

A birthday is a special day.

Birthdays are a time to say,
(Point to imaginary watch on wrist)

HAPPY BIRTHDAY!
(Everyone yell together)

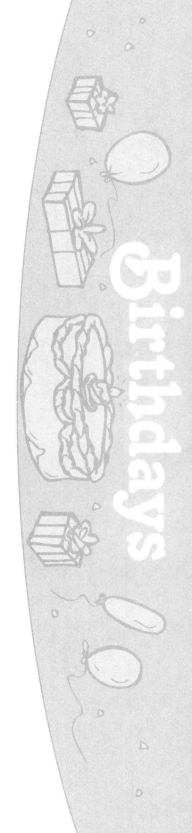

Party Hat Chat

I put on my party hat and took a bow;
(Touch head and bow)

I even put one on my favorite cow.
(Place hat on imaginary cow)

I put one on a duck and a sheep as well;
(Place hats on duck and sheep)

I put one on a horse called Belle.
(Place hat on horse)

Cow said, "My party hat is very tall."
(Stretch arms to ceiling)

Duck said, "My party hat is much too small."
(Crouch to floor)

Sheep said, "My party hat is rather wide!"
(Extend arms widely)

Horse said, "Mine fell over to the side!"
(Lean to one side)

I took off my party hat and said good-bye;
(Take hat off head)

I waved to the animals and winked my eye!
(Wave and wink)

Where Is My Piñata?

Where has my piñata gone?
(Place hands above eyes and look around)

I haven't seen it for so long!
(Place palms up)

Is it under my bed?
(Pretend to look under a bed)

Is it behind my head?
(Turn around)

Is it under my shoe?
(Look under shoe)

Is it under you?
(Look under a friend)

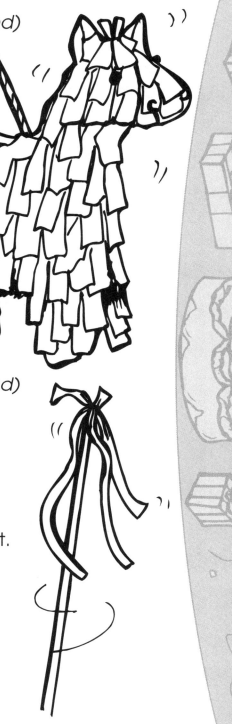

Where has my piñata gone?
(Place hands above eyes and look around)

I haven't seen it for so long!
(Place palms up)

I want to take a stick and hold it tight,
(Pretend to hold stick)

Then swing at the piñata with all my might.
(Swing arms)

It will break open and toys will fall out;
(Children may scramble to the floor)

We'll jump for joy and scream and shout.
(Jump two times)

Where has my piñata gone?
(Place hands above eyes and look around)

Wait! It was hanging from the ceiling all along!
(Point up)

Birthday Presents

I had a box to open.
(Pretend to open box)

Inside there was a surprise,
(Look surprised)

I wondered what it was—
(Scratch head)

A hamburger or fries?
(Rub tummy)

I ripped open the paper,
(Pretend to rip)

And what did I see?
(Point to eyes)

I saw a great big alligator
(Extend arms)

And a huge palm tree.
(Look up)

Then out came a swimming pool
(Swim)

And a diving board of course.
(Pretend to dive)

I could hardly believe it,
(Point to eyes)

But then I saw a giant horse!
(Extend arms)

He was holding an ice-cream cone
(Pretend to lick)

That had three giant scoops,
(Extend arms)

A double-decker sandwich
(Pretend to bite)

And a big bowl of soup.
(Pretend to slurp)

Then I had to close the box;
(Pretend to close)

It was too much of a surprise!
(Open eyes widely, place open hands around mouth)

I wrapped it up again,
(Pretend to wrap)

And then I blinked my eyes!
(Blink)

Balloon Broom

Once I had a big round balloon;
(Stretch arms to the side)

It was as big as the moon.
(Point up)

I used it as a broom
(Make sweeping motions)

To sweep my messy room.
(Keep sweeping)

I swept the kitchen and under my bed;
(Sweep)

I swept the hallway and over my head.
(Swing arms downwards, then above head)

When it touched the ceiling, it made a big pop!
(Jump)

Air flew at me, and I saw the balloon drop.
(Run then drop to floor)

It fell like a parachute to the floor,
(Jump up, then down)

So I blew up another balloon near the door.
(Make blowing motions with mouth)

I blew up a pink balloon so it was big;
(Stretch arms widely)

It looked like a farmyard pig.
(Move like a pig on the floor)

This time my balloon wasn't my broom;
(Shake finger)

It became a hanging mobile for my room!
(Point up)

Italian Pizza Swirls

Have you ever seen an Italian Pizza Swirl?
(Spin around)

It goes round and round like a curl.
(Twist arms, then legs)

It has red sauce in the center and is covered with cheese.
(Stretch arms out)

Let's make some together, please.
(Rub tummy)

First we'll knead a pile of dough,
(Pretend to knead)

Then cover it up and let it grow.
(Use arms to show growing)

Punch it down as hard as you can,
(Make punching motion)

Then roll it out to flatten.
(Make rolling motions)

Spread the sauce and sprinkle the cheese,
(Make spreading and sprinkling motions)

Roll it up like a blanket and be sure not to sneeze.
(Pretend to sneeze)

Cut it into pieces and place it on a pan,
(Pretend to divide the pizza)

And let it bake. Be patient if you can.
(Hands on hips, then tap foot)

Take it out of the oven and let it cool,
(Pretend to take from oven)

Then wrap it up and take it to school!
(Rub tummy)

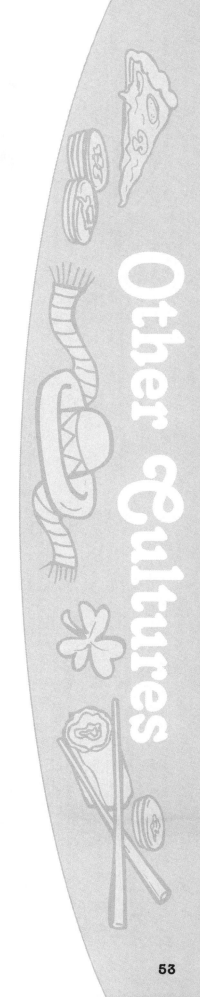

Other Cultures

Japanese Sushi Rolling Moves

If you're making sushi at school, the following poem will complement the activity.

Let's make sushi and roll it around.
(Roll around on mat)

Be careful not to drop it on the ground.
(Pretend to roll off a plate)

Let's roll to the left and roll to the right;
(Roll left and right on the floor)

Let's roll up and down and out of sight!
(Roll, then jump up and down)

First we spread the seaweed, then the rice,
(Pretend to spread ingredients)

And flatten it down to make it nice.
(Pat down with hand)

Fill it with cucumber, salmon or egg,
(Pretend to fill)

Then roll it up so it looks like a leg.
(Point to your leg)

Serve it in pieces like little pies.
(Pretend to share the pieces)

Sushi is a feast for the tummy and eyes!
(Point to tummy, then eyes)

Mexican Fiesta

Suggestion: Play a simple Mexican song in the background for this poem. Discuss the meanings of the Spanish words.

Where's your *sombrero*? Let's put it on.
(Place sombrero on head)

We'll strum our guitar to a Mexican song.
(Pretend or strum a real guitar)

Sing of *haciendas* and hot summer nights,
(Wipe your forehead)

Of warm beaches and stars that are bright,
(Hug yourself then point up)

Of plowing fields and the dancing *fiestas*,
(Dance a few steps)

And the quiet times for *siestas*.
(Place head in hands and close eyes)

Let's clap to the beat of the Mexican song,
(Clap)

Clap to the rhythm and sing along!
(Clap or sing)

Other Cultures

Croatian Breakfast

A Croatian pancake is thin and fluffy. It's also crispy because it's cooked in olive oil. A Croatian pancake is called a palacinka.

When I was a little kid, my breakfast wasn't plain;
(Place palms down)

'Twas Croatian style pancakes again and again.
(Pretend to flip pancakes)

My dad would put rosehip jam inside.
(Pretend to spread the jam)

He would roll them up with pride,
(Lift head)

Then he'd place them on my plate,
(Pretend to place pancakes on plate)

And I would savor every bite I ate.
(Make chewing motions)

I'd share them with my sister and brother;
(Pretend to pass out pancakes)

'Twas a family gathering like no other.
(Stretch arms out)

You should try these pancakes too;
(Rub tummy)

There will be enough for all of you.
(Cheer)

Note: You can make a batch for the classroom. Roll up the pancakes, cut them into sections and let children taste!

You Will Need

4 eggs, beaten
1 1/2 cups whole-wheat flour
2 cups milk
1/2 cup water
1 tsp. salt

Beat ingredients together. Add more water if needed. Heat olive oil on medium heat. Add batter, 1/4 cup at a time. Cook until golden on both sides. Serve with maple syrup or rosehip jam. Makes 8 pancakes.

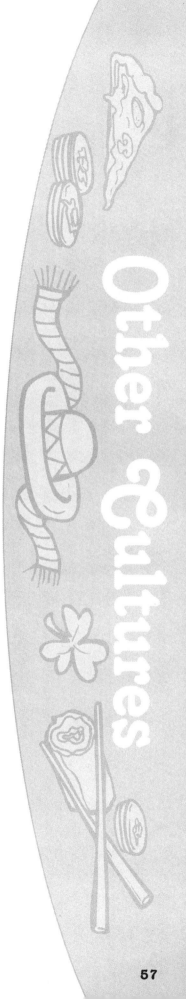

Other Cultures

Irish Soda Bread Feast

A girl named Mary baked Irish soda bread.
(Place "bread" in oven)

She kneaded the dough and got flour on her head.
(Wipe forehead)

You could smell the bread from miles around
(Lift nose in the air)

As the aroma danced through the town.
(Dance a few steps)

Boys and girls lined up in a row,
(Have children line up)

And went wherever the aroma would blow.
(Walk around the room)

They followed it high and followed it low,
(Reach high then crouch low)

And through the town that was below.
(Point to an imaginary town)

When they reached Mary's house they took a break,
(Keep walking)

And danced an Irish dance while the soda bread baked.
(Dance a few steps)

When it was done, everyone had a bite,
(Make biting motions)

Mary waved from her window and said "Good night!"
(Wave)

You're Number One!

It's possible to be number one;
(Place one finger up)

Stand up straight to see how it's done.
(Stand straight)

Stand like a soldier. Stand up tall.
(Stretch)

Make a "one" leaning against the wall.
(Stand against wall)

Make a "one" on the floor;
(Lie on floor)

Make a "one" against the door.
(Stand against door)

Make a "one" up in the air;
(Jump)

Make a "one" with your hair.
(Lift hair or trace with hair)

Make a "one" with your toes;
(Point toes)

Make a "one" with your nose.
(Lift nose up, then down)

Let's make a "one" across the room;
(Run across room)

Let's make a "one" while we zoom!
(Zoom across room)

You can see how much fun

It is to be number one!
(Lift one finger)

Two and Three!

Numbers two and three;
(Show two fingers then three)

That's what I like to see.
(Smile)

Make a two in the air;
(Use fingers to make a 2)

Trace a three on a pear.
(Use fingers to make a 3)

Step over two stones;
(Jump twice)

Grab two ice-cream cones.
(Pretend to pick up two cones)

Make a three on the floor,
(Lie down)

Make a three on the door.
(Stand against door)

Make a three on the wall;
(Lean against wall)

Make a three that's very tall.
(Stretch)

Numbers two and three;
(Hold two and three fingers up)

That's what I like to see!
(Point to self)

TLC10546 Copyright © Teaching & Learning Company, Carthage, IL 62321-001

Four and Five!

Once I knew a letter four;
(Hold up four fingers)

It came knocking at my door.
(Pretend to knock)

It jumped inside my house;
(Jump)

It was quiet like a mouse.
(Put finger in front of mouth)

We sat and sipped some tea;
(Pretend to sip)

Then it wanted to count with me.
(Count)

One, Two, Three, Four;
(Count)

Look who's coming through the door.
(Point)

It's our friend Number Five.
(Hold up five fingers)

What's in his hands? It's a beehive!
(Hold hands up)

He wants to pretend he is a bee,
("Buzz" like a bee)

And buzz around like this, you see.
(Keep buzzing)

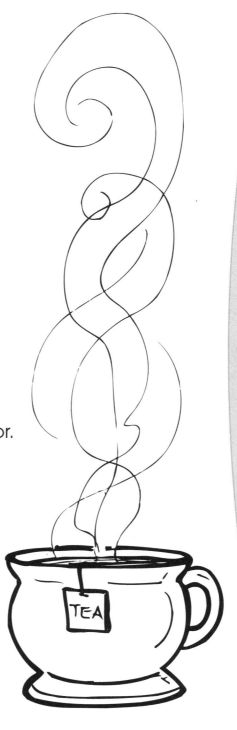

I said, "First, let's drink some tea!
(Pretend to drink tea)

And then you can count with me!"
(Count)

One, Two, Three, Four, Five!
(Count again)

Look what's coming out of the hive!
(Point and jump)

Bees were buzzing all around;
(Spin around)

They were making buzzing sounds.
(Make "buzzing" sounds)

"Help! Help!" said four and five.
(Yell "Help")

"Let's get rid of this beehive!"
(Pretend to throw hive)

Four and five ran out the door;
(Run across room)

Five said, "I won't bring hives anymore!"
(Wipe forehead)

Six, Seven and Eight!

Where are my friends six, seven and eight?
(Hold up six, seven and then eight fingers)

They are always really late!
(Point at clock)

They were late for breakfast and brunch,
(Look sad)

But here they are on time for lunch!
(Jump up and down)

Let's do some counting before we eat;
(Count to six, seven then eight)

Let's count the toes on our feet.
(Count toes)

Let's count the glasses and then the plates,
(Count glasses, then plates)

And after lunch, we'll count what we ate.
(Count again)

Counting is so much fun!
(Jump up and down)

We'll take a bow when we are done!
(Bow)

Numbers

1 2 3 4 5 6 7 8 9 10

Nine and Ten!

When I was nine, I counted sheep;
(Count pretend sheep)

Counting them put me right to sleep.
(Place head in hands)

I counted donkeys and horses too;
(Count pretend donkeys and horses)

I counted animals found in a zoo.
(List zoo animals)

I counted the monkeys and elephants too;
(Look at pictures of monkeys and elephants)

I counted all the peacocks as they flew.
(Wave arms as if flying)

I counted to number ten
(Count to ten together)

By counting llamas in their pen.
(Count llamas in a picture)

I counted ten hungry boars,
(Rub tummy)

I counted ten gorillas that snore.
(Snore)

When I was only nine I used to count some sheep;
(Count to ten)

Counting them put me right to sleep!
(Place head in hands)